DATE DUE

Jun 26'84			
Jul 10'84			
Ju 16'85			

LITTLE GIANTS

by Seymour Simon

*illustrated
by Pamela Carroll*

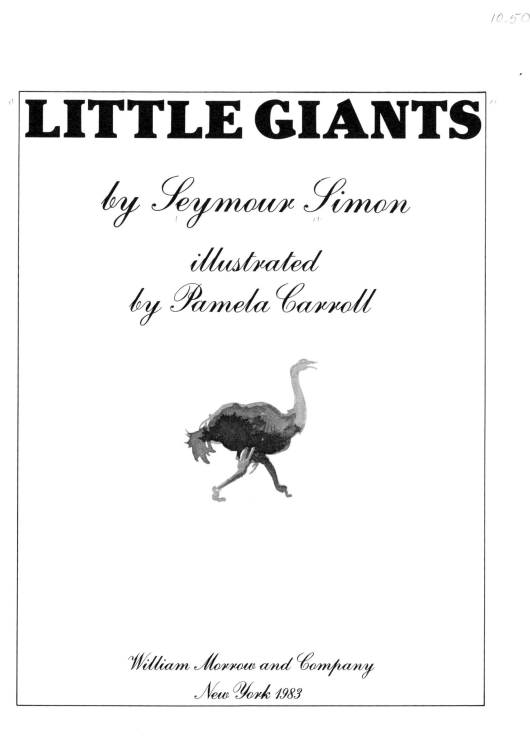

*William Morrow and Company
New York 1983*

To Lucy Martin Bitzer

INTRODUCTION

*H*OW BIG IS A GIANT: TEN FEET TALL? FIFTY FEET? ONE hundred feet? Can you imagine a giant only a few feet tall? Or one only a few inches long? It all depends upon the animal you are talking about. ❧ An ant is usually quite small—about one-quarter inch long. An ant more than one inch long is a giant ant. ❧ Most insects weigh only a fraction of an ounce, so an insect that weighs a quarter of a pound is a giant insect. ❧ You can easily lift most freshwater fish. But a freshwater fish that weighs thirty times as much as you do is a giant fish. ❧ This book is about these "little" giants. Some are only a few inches long. A few are bigger than you are. But all of them are truly giants when compared to others of their kind.

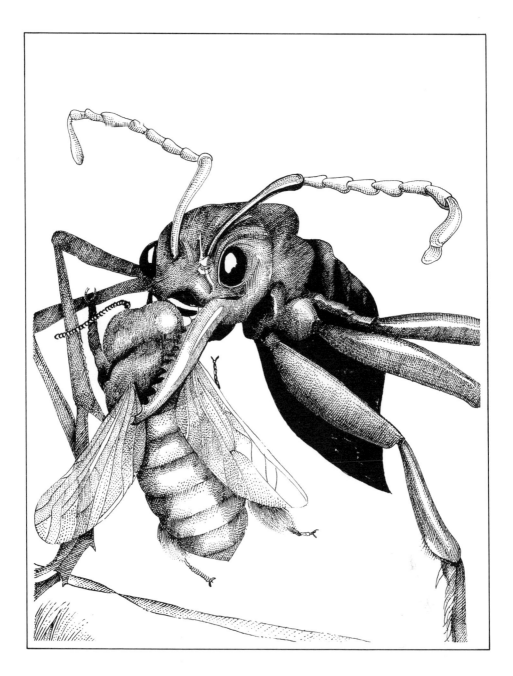

Bulldog Ants

THE BULLDOG ANTS OF AUSTRALIA ARE AMONG THE largest of all ants. Some of the workers measure nearly one and one-half inches long, about six times the size of the common household ant. ✻ Not only are bulldog ants large, but they also have powerful jaws and a powerful sting, which they don't hesitate to use on anything that bothers them, including human beings. In fact, bulldog ants will chase humans who come within thirty feet of their nests. ✻ Worker ants usually hunt singly for insect prey. The ants move very rapidly over the ground and on low-growing plants. They have large eyes and good vision as well as a keen sense of smell. The bulldog hunters run quickly, and they can leap several inches when they attack. ✻ The ants are good hunters. They are even able to pull down and kill bees and other powerful insects. The insects are first paralyzed by the ant's sting and then cut up by its jaws and fed to the ant young. The workers also collect flower nectar, which they use in their diet. ✻ A bulldog ant colony ranges in size from a few hundred to about one thousand workers. Approaching a nest can be dangerous. Bulldog ants will attack humans using their stings and jaws. In some cases, people have even died after being stung and bitten by these ants.

Robber Flies

ROBBER FLIES HAVE TO BE APPROACHED WITH CAUTION. These little monsters are over two inches long, and can give you a painful bite. The largest have wingspans of nearly four inches. With their legs extended they measure more than seven inches. By comparison, a housefly is about one-quarter inch long. ✿ Few flying insects are safe from attacks by robber flies, not even bees and wasps. A great flyer, the robber fly overtakes its prey in the air and seizes it with its six powerful legs. At the same time, the fly jabs its poisonous beak into the soft neck of its victim. In an instant the bee or wasp stops struggling. Then the robber fly lands at some convenient spot to suck its prey dry. ✿ The largest kinds of robber flies live in tropical South America and Australia, but there are many large kinds that live in the United States. In many areas you can find them flying over open, sunny fields. Some kinds are gold and black and look like bumblebees. Other kinds are black, brown, and reddish. They are usually covered with stubby bristles. ✿ The robber fly is a fierce hunter even when it is a newly hatched larva. The larva searches through rotting wood and piles of decaying leaves for insects and other small, soft-bodied creatures.

The Giant Water Bug

*T*O MANY PEOPLE, THE WORD "BUG" MEANS ANY INSECT that they don't like. To a scientist, true bugs are a certain group of insects, the *Hemiptera* (which means "half-wings"). 🦋 The giant water bug is the largest water bug in the world. Some kinds living in tropical places reach lengths of five to six inches. In the United States giant water bugs are rarely over three and a half inches. 🦋 Some people call giant water bugs "toe biters." The giants are dark-colored and almost invisible as they lie half-buried in the mud at the bottom of a pond. The bugs reach out to grab anything that comes near, from an insect to a fish to a swimmer's toe. 🦋 With human beings the bugs can deliver a painful but not fatal bite. With insects or fish, the bugs jab again and again with their beaks until the victim is dead. A giant water bug can kill a fish twice its size. 🦋 At night, the giant water bugs may leave their ponds and fly off. Sometimes they are attracted to lights near the water. If they crawl in an open window to get at a light they will start to thrash against the walls and ceilings trying to escape. Imagine how you would feel if you saw this huge bug flying around your living room!

The Mysterious Lantern Fly

OF SOUTH AMERICA MAY BE THE

int bugs. It is about three inches long

e its length. The lantern fly is also

g or the peanut bug. That's because

ooks like an alligator or a pea-

iis bug's head is hollow like a shell.

o benefit the lantern fly at all, or at

id out. Another of the mysteries

s name of lantern fly. It seems that

ntist who saw the heads of these

were usually very accurate, but

ly glow. It is still an unsolved

itern flies that live in the tropics.

t hardens in the air. This often

ls. No one is quite sure

ds. In fact, we don't

antern fly. It is

giant.

The Heaviest Insect

Butterflies as Big as Birds

THE GOLIATH BEETLE OF WEST AFRICA IS THE HEAVIEST insect in the world. The large adults are over four inches long and weigh nearly a quarter of a pound. Despite their size and weight, goliath beetles are able to fly. These little giants fly like bullets and can crash through glass windows. ✿ Most of the time, the goliaths hang like monkeys from the branches of palm trees, eating the buds and damaging the trees. The powerful insects encircle the branches with their front legs, which are used almost like arms. Their hold is so tight that they seem attached to the tree. It is almost impossible to tear a goliath loose without cutting your hand. ✿ The male goliath is velvety and reddish-brown with a beautiful white design on its back. It has a large frontward-pointing horn coming from the back of its head. The males fight one another. They try to catch their opponents with the horn and then flip them into the air with a toss of their heads. ✿ The horn is not of much use against other kinds of enemies, however. Instead, the goliath has a concealed trap. It opens a sharp-edged joint between its chest shield and its wing covers. This can snap shut powerfully on any enemy such as a bird, and could easily snap off a leg.

THE BIRDWING BUTTERFLIES OF THE SOUTH PACIFIC AND the giant swallowtail butterfly of Africa are the biggest butterflies in the world. These colorful giants have wing spans of eight to eleven inches. ✺ When these butterflies fly around the tops of tall trees, they look like birds in flight. They are rapid fliers and are very difficult for collectors to catch. Instead of using nets to snare them, collectors try to knock the butterflies down with blasts of water. Can you imagine going butterfly hunting with a water pistol? ✺ There is another kind of giant swallowtail that is the largest butterfly in the United States. Its wings span more than five inches across. Swallowtails have strong wings that can take them straight up in the air. Catching a swallowtail is not an easy job for a collector. ✺ The giant swallowtail's wings are black on top with rows of yellow spots near the edges. The undersides of the wings are yellow. The swallowtails live from Florida and Texas north to the Canadian border. ✺ The swallowtail caterpillar is about two and one-half inches long. In the north the caterpillars feed on prickly ash and hop trees. In the south they feed on orange trees, often doing much damage. Fruit growers call this caterpillar the "orange dog."

The Giant Earthworm

IMAGINE GOING FISHING WITH AN ELEVEN-FOOT EARTHWORM! That's the size of some of the giant earthworms that live in Australia. The giants may weigh up to one and one-half pounds. 🌿 Capturing one of the giants is quite a trick. You have to dig into their burrows until you find enough of a worm exposed. Then you grab the worm and quickly tie a knot in it. Otherwise it will disappear down its hole in an instant. 🌿 When you first grab this worm, it sprays a milky fluid in all directions for about a foot. The fluid comes out of pores along the worm's body. It is usually given off by the worm in the soil to make the burrow easier to crawl through. 🌿 You can't just grab a giant worm and start pulling. The giant expands its body inside the curving burrow and hangs onto the sides so tightly that the piece you hold will come right off in your hand. 🌿 You have to have patience. You can dig the rest of the worm out following its twisting burrow. Or you can try easing the giant worm out of its burrow, inch by inch, pulling it out slowly but steadily. 🌿 That's the way the kookaburra bird captures the worm. This sharp-eyed bird spots part of a worm from the air and dives down. Grabbing a piece of the worm with its beak, the bird braces itself and waits. Each time the worm eases up an instant, the bird gives a quick tug and takes up the slack. Finally the worm weakens and the last inches slip out. But the bird can't fly away with its catch, because the worm is too heavy. 🌿 The bulging head-end of the worm has a slit of a mouth, a quarter of an inch wide. The worm tunnels through the ground, swallowing soil and passing it through its body. The egg capsules of the giants are laid in the soil or among the roots of plants. A just-hatched baby worm measures about six inches in length!

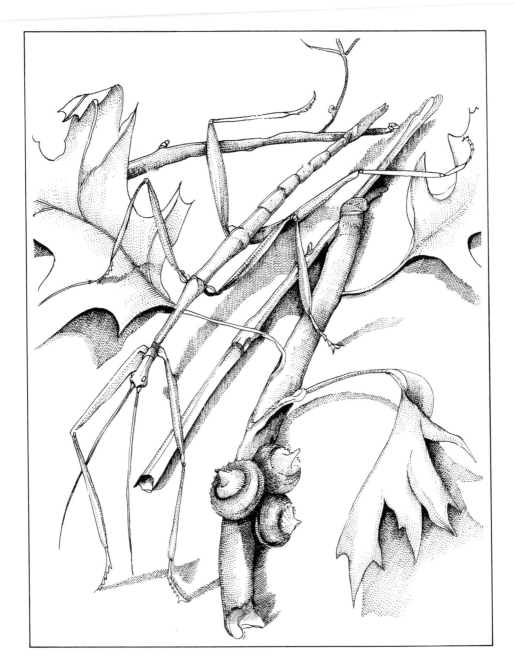

The Longest Insects

WALKINGSTICK INSECTS ARE LONG AND THIN. SOME are flattened and look like a leaf. Others are thin and stretched out and look like twigs. All walkingsticks are at least several inches long. The largest walkingsticks are found in southeast Asia. Some of those are over one foot in length. 🍃 Walkingsticks feed and move about at night. They move slowly and clumsily as they eat the green leaves of trees and other plants. A walkingstick stays stiff and rigid like a dead piece of wood. But every once in a while it will sway back and forth as though blown by a breeze. 🍃 Walkingsticks are usually the same color as their surroundings: gray, brown, or green. Most can even change colors slowly from brown to green and back again. Their enemies—lizards, birds, and spiders—have a difficult time seeing them unless they move. 🍃 During the day walkingsticks remain absolutely rigid and motionless. In fact, they seem to be in some kind of trancelike state. You can move their legs into any position and they will remain there. 🍃 The "laboratory" stick is an Asian walkingstick that is often kept in laboratories or as a pet. It is very easy to keep and breed as long as it is kept warm. It can be fed on many kinds of green leaves.

Dragons of the Insect World

A SUMMER DAY AT A POND IS THE TIME AND PLACE TO SEE the flying dragons of the insect world, the dragonflies.

Many common kinds of dragonflies in the United States have wingspans of three or four inches. The largest tropical dragonflies living today have wingspans of more than seven inches. But even these are small compared to the ancestors of dragonflies that lived millions of years ago. Fossils have been discovered that show dragonflies with a wing spread of two and a half feet! The dragonfly is one of the best flyers in the world of nature. It can fly frontwards, backwards, straight up like a rocket, and even stop and turn on a dime. A big dragonfly can reach speeds of more than fifty miles per hour. Many dragonflies are in the air almost constantly during daylight hours. Some species catch mostly mosquitos, other kinds go for butterflies and moths. A dragonfly catches its prey with its legs as if in a basket. Then it brings the prey instantly to its mouth, which has sharp, knifelike pincers. The glittering eyes of a dragonfly are excellent for a hunter. Each eye is made up of ten thousand or more lenses. The head is also moveable. This gives the dragonfly a huge field of vision—all the better to see and attack its prey.

The Bird-Eating Spider

MAGINE A HAIRY SPIDER LARGER THAN YOUR HAND THAT CAN catch and eat animals as big as hummingbirds. This is the bird-eating spider of South America—the biggest spider in the world. These giant spiders are found around the Amazon River basin. Their bodies can reach a length of more than three inches with a leg span of more than ten inches. The body and legs of the bird-eating spider are hairy, and the hairs are irritating to human skin—that is, if you ever care to handle one of them! The bite is only slightly poisonous, but it can cause pain and swelling in humans. During daylight hours, the bird-eating spider remains in a hole in the ground or in a tree. At night it comes out to hunt. This spider does not spin a web. Rather, it captures its prey by creeping up and then springing with a sudden dash. It catches small mammals such as mice and birds, as well as all kinds of insects. Once the spider captures its prey, it injects a fluid that turns its victim's body into a liquid that the spider sucks out. The bird-eating spider has few natural enemies, probably because its body hairs are so irritating to the touch. Its main enemies are hunting wasps. These insects sting the spider and paralyze it. Then they store the body in an underground nest, where the wasp larvae feed upon it.

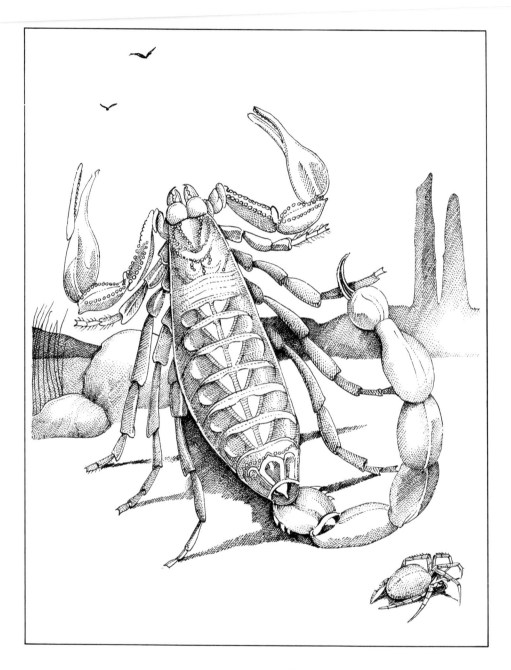

The Giant Scorpions

SCORPIONS ARE FAMOUS FOR THE POISONOUS STINGS AT the ends of their tails. The stinger is used both to defend the scorpion from its enemies and to quiet struggling victims that it intends to eat.　Most kinds of scorpions in the southwestern United States are two or three inches long or less. But several have stings which are very dangerous to people. A sting from one of these dangerous species can cause vomiting, difficulty in breathing, and even death. In fact, more people in the United States and Mexico are killed by scorpions than by snakes.　The American scorpions are small compared to the seven- to eight-inch African scorpions. These have large stingers and plentiful poison, and they can easily deliver a sting fatal to a person. The lobster-scorpions of Sumatra are said to be even larger, perhaps over ten inches long, but little is known about these forest dwellers.　Scorpions hunt for insects and spiders at night. They seize their victims with their large claws. Then they tear them to pieces or crush them. Only if their victims offer resistance do scorpions use their stings.　Scorpions are found in warm places all around the world. They are plentiful in the southwestern United States and Mexico. But they are also found as far north as British Columbia in Canada.　In some places the number of scorpions is greater than the number of people. In one area of Bombay, India, a casual hunt revealed fifteen thousand scorpions in a place where thirteen thousand people lived.

The Flying Fox

THE FLYING FOX IS THE BIGGEST BAT IN THE WORLD. IT has a wingspan of over five feet and a body length of more than one foot, about five times the wingspan of the common brown bat. The flying fox is dark gray or black, with yellow or tan markings on its shoulders. Its face is like a fox's with a long, slender muzzle. As frightening as it may look, the flying fox feeds mostly on fruit. The other item in its diet is small fish. The giant bats fly low over the water and catch fish with their feet. Then they fly to a nearby tree to eat their catch. Flying foxes are social animals, staying together in great numbers during daylight hours. A single tree may sometimes be home to a colony of hundreds of bats. At sundown, all the bats leave their tree roost and wing their way into the night sky. In their search for food, the bats hunt by themselves rather than in a group.

When they return to their tree after feeding, each bat tries to get its favorite spot. The bats must be evenly spaced so that they do not touch each other, so there is a great deal of quarreling and commotion as they settle down for the day. They hang from branches by one or two feet with their heads on their chests and partly covered by folded wings.

Flying foxes live in tropical Asia, the islands of the South Pacific, and eastern Australia. Sometimes they go on seasonal migrations, traveling north or south in huge flocks.

The Giant Snail

OST LAND SNAILS THAT YOU MIGHT FIND UNDER A pile of decaying leaves are less than an eighth of an inch long and weigh only a fraction of an ounce. But one land snail that comes from East Africa is a giant among snails. An average giant snail weighs half a pound and is eight inches long! And some snails twice that size have been found. ✌ The giant snail has spread from East Africa to many of the warmer parts of the world, including India, the Far East, the South Pacific, and even the United States. Sometimes the snail was accidentally brought into a country in a shipment of fruit or soil. At other times the snail was deliberately introduced. For example, the Japanese soldiers took snails along as food during the Second World War. In its original land, the giant snail was not a pest. But in many other countries it became a great nuisance. ✌ The giant snail feeds not only on rotting plants but also on the leaves, fruit, and flowers of living plants such as beans, citrus trees, melons, and rubber trees. It may even eat the whitewash off the walls of houses. ✌ The snail also multiplies very rapidly. It can lay several hundred pea-sized eggs in the soil every two or three months. The young hatch in just a few days. In a year, they are also laying eggs.

The result is that a single snail can have millions of descendants in less than a decade.

The Giant Salamander

THE GIANT SALAMANDER LIVES IN MOUNTAIN STREAMS IN China and Japan. The largest ones are over five feet long and weigh nearly one hundred pounds. They are so large that they are used as food by the natives. But these giants are becoming rare because they grow so slowly and are usually captured and killed before they reach full size.　Salamanders are related to frogs and toads. They are all amphibians—animals that live both on land and in water. The easiest way to tell salamanders from frogs and toads is that all salamanders have tails. Most salamanders are just a few inches long.　The giant salamander lays her eggs in the water in what looks like strings of beads. The young, called larvae, have gills when they hatch. The larvae keep their gills for nearly three years. Although they still spend all their time in the water, the adults develop lungs and must come to the surface to breathe.　The only close relative of the giant salamander is the hellbender, which lives in some of the rivers in the eastern part of the United States. The hellbender is the largest amphibian in North America. It can grow to more than two feet in length.

Giant salamanders are very long lived. Some have been kept alive in zoos for as long as fifty years. Hellbenders are also long lived. One hellbender lived for twenty-nine years in captivity.

The Marine Toad

OST TOADS CAN FIT IN THE PALM OF YOUR HAND. But not the marine or giant toad. A large female marine toad can be more than nine inches long and six inches across with its legs folded. It weighs more than two pounds.   The giant toad can be found over a wide range from southern Texas and Florida through Mexico and Central America down to South America. The biggest toads are found in Central and South America. In Texas and Florida, the largest ones are about seven inches long.   The giant toad has very large poison glands located over its shoulders. If the toad is bothered or attacked, a milky poison oozes from the pores of the gland. The taste of the poison discourages most enemies from bothering the toad any further.

The giant toad has been introduced into many areas by people to control insects. In particular, the toad has been useful in eating insects that infest sugar cane plantations. The toad lives around houses, gardens, fields, and ponds. During the day, it usually hides under rocks or logs or in holes in the ground. At night, it comes out to feed. In the tropics, it sings in large groups.

A Giant Rodent

MAGINE A PET GUINEA PIG GROWN TO THE SIZE OF A REAL PIG. That's what the capybara looks like. It is the largest rodent in the world. A full-grown adult capybara is four feet long and two feet high at the shoulder. Its weight can reach over one hundred and fifty pounds. ❦ The capybara is sometimes called the "giant water guinea pig." It makes its home among the tall grasses along the banks of South American rivers. It is a good swimmer and feeds on water plants, grasses, and other plants. Its hairy coat ranges from brown to reddish-yellow. ❦ Even though the capybara is very large, it runs from its enemies rather than fight them. It is always on the alert for a jaguar or cougar. At the first sign of one of these big cats the capybara leaps into the water. It can swim underwater for long distances. But even in the water the capybara must be alert for another enemy, the alligator. ❦ Capybaras often travel around in families or troops. Their families are large; four to eight babies are born in a litter. The babies are well developed and can soon take care of themselves. ❦ South American natives hunt the capybara in canoes. They kill it when it comes up for air. They eat its flesh and make ornaments of its large teeth. You may not be able to see a capybara in the wild, but many zoos around the world have capybaras in their collections.

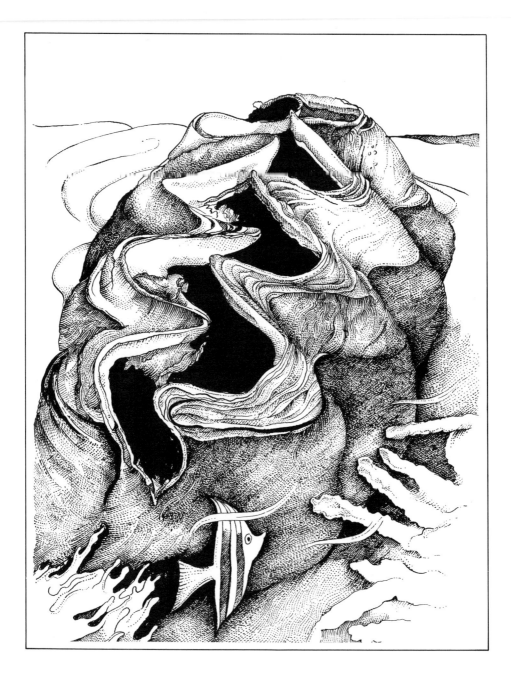

The Giant Clam

THE GIANT CLAM HAS A SHELL THAT CAN BE MORE THAN four feet long and weigh more than five hundred pounds. The soft parts of a giant clam weigh about twenty pounds —enough for a lot of clam chowder. These clams live in the warm waters around Australia, many South Pacific islands, and the east coast of Africa. The giant clam is the largest clam in the world. It is sometimes called the killer clam or the man-eating clam. The names come from stories about divers who drowned after getting a foot caught between the close-fitting shells of the clam. Is the giant clam really a killer? It certainly could be. The two shells fit together tightly. A diver could easily put his foot into an open clam. The clam shells close so slowly that there is plenty of time for the diver to remove his leg. Once the clam does close, however, a diver would not have the strength to pull it apart. There are many stories about people being trapped by the clams, but none of the stories has been proved beyond a doubt. The clam does not clamp down on large animals when it eats. Despite its large size, the giant clam feeds in the same way that smaller clams do. It opens its shell and filters microscopic plants and animals from the ocean water. If the giant clam does trap people or a large animal, it is just a defensive reflex. It will not eat them.

Big Bird

THE LARGEST OF LIVING BIRDS IS THE AFRICAN OSTRICH. It stands seven to nine feet tall and can weigh over three hundred pounds. Giant flightless birds called moas that weighed five hundred pounds, once lived in New Zealand. But a few hundred years ago the last ones were killed off by humans. Ostriches live on the African plains along with grazing animals such as zebras and antelope, and preying animals such as lions and cheetahs. Though unable to fly, the ostrich is not helpless against its enemies. It has a twelve-foot stride which carries it along at forty miles an hour—fast enough to outrace most pursuers. Its long legs can deliver a kick that is said to be more powerful than a mule's. Its height and good vision allow it to sense danger from far away. Male ostriches are handsome birds, with fluffy black and white feathers that are some-times used for people's hats or clothing. The female ostrich is a darker brown and a bit smaller than the male. Ostriches eat almost any-thing—plants, small animals, and even bits of broken rock. Ostriches kept in captivity will eat anything from bottles and watches to golf balls and jewelry. A female ostrich lays about fifteen white eggs in a shallow nest dug in the ground. Each egg weighs about three pounds.

It takes six weeks for the ostrich chicks to hatch.

With their prickly, stiff down feathers, the

large chicks look like porcupines.

The Giant Tortoise

TORTOISES ARE TURTLES THAT LIVE ON THE LAND. THE largest tortoises in the world are found on the Galapagos Islands in the Pacific Ocean off the coast of Ecuador. These giant tortoises can weigh more than four hundred pounds and have shells of four feet in length. The giant tortoises of the Galapagos feed mostly on cactus and grass. They move slowly and are quite harmless. For protection they depend upon their shells and their size. Unfortunately, the arrival of humans on the Galapagos Islands has cut back on their numbers. Hundreds of the tortoises were killed for their oil. Pigs and dogs dug up their eggs to eat. Tortoises have been killed off on some of the smaller islands. The giant tortoises lay small numbers of eggs, usually less than twenty. The eggs are round, white-shelled and about two and one-half inches around. The tortoises do not breed in captivity. Young tortoises grow rapidly, sometimes doubling their weight every year. One tortoise went from twenty-nine pounds to three hundred and fifty pounds in seven years. If left alone, giant tortoises can live for a very long time, longer than all other animals with backbones. Records show that some have lived more than one hundred years and possibly more than one hundred fifty years. Reports of tortoises living for as long as three hundred years are very doubtful.

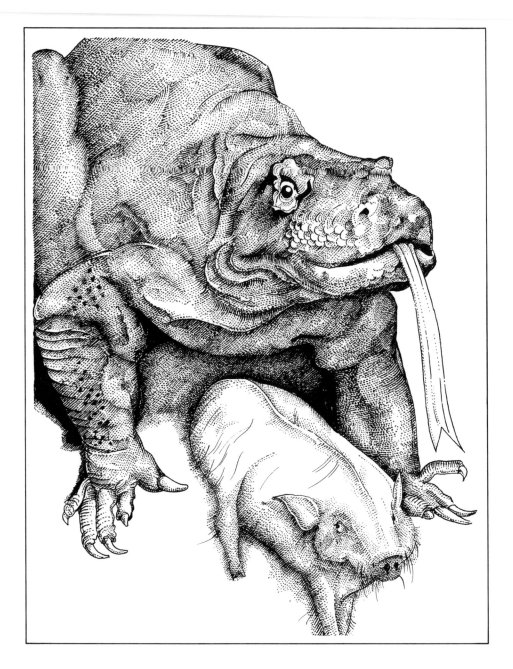

The Komodo Dragon

KOMODO IS A SMALL, MOUNTAINOUS VOLCANIC ISLAND that is part of Indonesia. On this island lives the largest lizard in the world—the Komodo dragon. The Komodo dragon is nearly ten feet long and weighs about two hundred pounds. The Komodo is a kind of lizard known as a monitor. Sixty million years ago monitor lizards lived in North America. Their fossil remains have been found in Wyoming. Nowadays, monitors are found only in parts of Asia, Africa, and Australia. The Komodo lives on a rocky island with some grass and only a few bushes and palm trees. The lizard walks with its body held well off the ground and its darting tongue constantly moving. Its tongue picks up the odors of the wild pigs and small deer that also live on the island. These animals are its main food. In the hot season, when the temperature can go to over 120° Fahrenheit, the dragons are on the move for only a few hours in the early morning. The rest of the time they stay in shady places where they shelter from the sun. Young dragons can climb trees, but the adults are too heavy. They visit water holes to drink and cool off, and they also swim in the surf on the beaches. Sometimes they swim through strong currents to nearby small islets where they attack domestic goats.

The Leatherback

THE LEATHERBACK—OR LEATHERY—TURTLE IS A REAL giant among sea turtles. Some leatherbacks grow to more than eight feet long and weigh nearly one ton. Their front flippers are very large. An average turtle may have flippers spanning nine feet.   The leatherback turtle gets its name from its upper shell. The shell is made up of hundreds of bony plates covered with a leathery skin. There are seven ridges running down its back and five ridges on the lower shell. Adult leathery turtles are dark brown or black.   Leatherback turtles are found in warmer oceans all around the world. The largest ones live in the Pacific Ocean. The Atlantic leatherback is rarely heavier than eight hundred pounds.

Not much is known about the habits and breeding places of the leatherbacks. They spend much of their time in deep waters, unseen by people. They are powerful swimmers and are sometimes escorted by pilot fish, which more commonly stay with sharks.   Female leathery turtles come ashore in small groups to lay their eggs, usually at night. They come straight out of the water and move up the beach until they reach dry sand. Then they stop and dig a hollow. After digging as deep as they can reach, they lay about 60 to 100 two-inch eggs, then fill the nest with sand and pack it down. The eggs hatch in about seven weeks. The babies immediately rush down the shore into the sea.

A Giant Fish

THE LARGEST FRESHWATER FISH IN THE WORLD IS THE Russian—or beluga—sturgeon. There is a record of one beluga that weighed 3,210 pounds and was more than twenty-four feet long! Female belugas sometimes contain huge amounts of small blackish eggs, or roe. The eggs are a rare food delicacy. They are cleaned and salted and then called caviar. Nowadays beluga caviar is sold for hundreds of dollars for just a few ounces. A female beluga once yielded four hundred pounds of caviar! Sturgeons are slow-moving fish, spending their time rooting along the river bottom for food. They find the food by touch, using their sensitive barbels, which look like whiskers. Sturgeons eat insect young, worms, snails, and small fishes. The beluga also swims out to sea in the winter to feed on flounder and other bottom dwellers. Two close relatives of the beluga are the Atlantic sturgeon and the white sturgeon. While not as large as the beluga, both can reach lengths of over ten feet and weights of over one thousand pounds. All three kinds of sturgeon have been overfished and are now relatively rare.

Printed in the United States of America
Book design by Lucy Martin Bitzer
1 2 3 4 5 6 7 8 9 10

LIBRARY OF CONGRESS CATALOGING IN PUBLICATION DATA

Simon, Seymour.
Little giants.
Summary: Text and illustrations describe the largest of the small creatures in the animal world, including the bulldog ant, goliath beetle, and the komodo dragon.
1. Animals—Miscellanea—Juvenile literature. 2. Body size—Juvenile literature.
[1. Animals. 2. Size and shape] I. Carroll, Pamela, ill. II. Title.
QL49.S5192   1982   591   82-14139
ISBN 0-688-01727-4
ISBN 0-688-01731-2 (lib. bdg.)